123760

OVID AND THE ELIZABETHANS

*A Lecture delivered at a Joint Meeting of the English Association
and the London Branch of the Classical Association*

By FREDERICK S. BOAS, HON. LL.D., HON. D.LITT., F.R.S.L.

IT has been my good fortune at sundry times to read papers or take the Chair at meetings of the English Association and of Branches of the Classical Association. But this is the first time that I have had the privilege of addressing the two bodies together. It is indeed, I believe, the first occasion of such a joint session. I hope and believe that it may be regardedi n Shakespearian words, as " the marriage of true minds."

I would like this paper to be considered in part a tribute to the memory of two distinguished men, to whom Classical and English literatures were equally dear—Dr J. W. Mackail and my brother-in-law, Dr S. G. Owen. Dr Mackail's eminent services to the classical cause have been eloquently commemorated by Sir Frank Fletcher in his 1946 presidential address to the Classical Association, and all who knew him would echo the words that his " character was permeated with the beauty of the poetry which he studied and interpreted." I first knew him when I was a freshman at Balliol, and he was one of a brilliant group of senior men who rose to eminence in letters and public life, in the Church and the law. In later life our chief contact was in the Elizabethan Literary Society, of which he was to the last a devoted member. It was he also who enlisted me in the ranks of the Classical Association, with the luring words that the subscription was only five shillings. His masterpiece in little on Latin literature has been my treasured possession since its appearance in 1895. He is one of the select few who have been Presidents of both the Classical and the English Associations, which jointly rejoiced when he received the Order of Merit.

Dr S. G. Owen was, like Mackail, a Balliol undergraduate, but after a short period as lecturer at Manchester he returned to Oxford as a senior student and classical tutor of Christ Church, of which he became a loyal adopted son. His special field was the Roman Augustan period, particularly Juvenal and Ovid, but the width of his interests was shown by his labours for a number of years as editor of *The Year's Work in Classical Studies*. In English literature his somewhat austere taste found its favourite reading in the eighteenth century. Was there not a sign of austerity too when, as a comparatively young man, he chose among Ovid's works the *Tristia* in 1889 for intensive editorial labours. In 1915 he contributed it with *Ibis* and the *Pontic Epistles* to the Oxford Classical Texts, and in 1924 he published the Second Book with a translation and commentary. Meanwhile, in 1912, he contributed an attractive essay on " Ovid and Romance " to the volume *English Literature and the Classics*, edited by G. S. Gordon, afterwards President of Magdalen.

We have thus been brought to the threshold of our subject this afternoon. Will the learned classicists present bear with me while for the sake of any who on this particular occasion may be among the weaker brethren I summarize briefly Ovid's career. Publius Ovidius Naso was born on March 20, 45 B.C., at Sulmo, about ninety miles east of Rome. His family were of equestrian rank, and he was destined by his father for a legal and public career. He did attain to some minor offices, but his training in rhetoric and literature was soon diverted to other than forensic ends. Like Pope he " lisped in numbers, for the numbers came." He himself tells that he was giving recitations of his youthful poem, the *Amores*, when his beard had been cut but once or twice. The immediate popularity won by this poem, together with his conversational and other gifts, at once secured for Ovid a distinguished place in Roman literary and social circles. He was married three times, the first two unions being short. The third, though childless, was one of mutual devotion.

The exact chronology of his writings is obscure. But the *Amores* was followed by the *Heroides*, a series of love-letters from legendary ladies of renown. Then came, about 1 B.C., the eventful *Ars Amatoria*, " a systematic treatise," as it has been described, " in voluptuous pleasure." As an antidote to the scandal that it aroused it was succeeded by the *Remedia Amoris*. In the second period of his literary career Ovid turned away from the erotic field in which he had so signally triumphed. In the *Metamorphoses* he achieved equal success in poetic narrative, which embodied a mass of mythological stories whose only connecting link was that they involved the transformation of human beings into some other shape. Of his major works *Metamorphoses* alone was written not in the elegiac metre but in hexameters. His other chief narrative work, the *Fasti*, based on the calendar of the months, and " a storehouse of religious and antiquarian lore," was less successful and was never published in complete form.

Then suddenly in A.D. 8 came a bolt from the blue. Augustus ordered the poet's banishment to Tomis, a small town in a desolate and bitterly cold region, about sixty-five miles south-west of the nearest mouth of the Danube. The cause of Ovid's ' relegatio,' technically the milder form of the penalty, has never been fully solved. He himself attributed it to a ' carmen ' (poem) and an ' error.' It is generally agreed that the ' carmen ' was the *Ars Amatoria* which the Emperor considered an obstacle to his plans for moral reformation in Rome. As to the ' error ' it was at one time thought that it had some relation to the profligacy of the Emperor's granddaughter, Julia, who was banished in the same year as Ovid. But it is now usually believed to have been not of a domestic but of a political nature. In any case Augustus, and after him Tiberius, was obdurate to the confessions of guilt and the pleas for mercy which poured from the desolate exile in his last group of poems, the *Tristia* and *Epistulae ex Ponto*. He had to linger on, heart-broken, till his death in A.D. 16 or 17.

But however tragic the close of his fortunes, Ovid's confidence that his fame would survive has been fully justified. Of his general European popularity in the Middle Ages this is not the occasion to speak. But in fourteenth-century England both Chaucer and Gower show his influence. Their respective debt to the *Metamorphoses* in their treatment of the Pyramus and Thisbe story in *The Legend of Good Women* and the *Confessio Amantis* has been recently discussed by Mr Norman Callan in *R.E.S.*, October 1946, as also other contrasted borrowings. The eagle that bears Chaucer to the House of Fame even calls the *Metamorphoses* ' thyne owne book,' but an unlearned reader would not grasp the allusion. The first attempt, so far as I know, to make any part of Ovid intelligible to the English laity in the vernacular was Wynkyn de Worde's publication in 1513 of *The flores of Ovide de arte amandi with theyr englysshe afore them*. This may have been something in the nature of a school-book like Nicholas Udall's *Floures for Latine spekyinge selected and gathered out of Terence* (1533), phrases from three plays of Terence with their English equivalents. Except, however, for Wynkyn de Worde's venture it was not Ovid who had the distinction of leading the way among the Latin poets in the great outburst of Tudor translation from the Classics. As all know, the priority fell to Virgil, when the ill-fated Henry Howard, Earl of Surrey, rendered Books II and IV of the *Aeneid* into the then unfamiliar metre which we now know as blank verse. The translation was published by Tottel in 1557 but probably dates not long before Surrey's execution early in 1548. Gawin Douglas's version of the whole poem in Scottish vernacular, though finished in 1513, was published in 1553. In 1558 there came from Thomas Phaer his rendering of the first seven Books of the *Aeneid* in fourteeners, followed in 1562 by the first nine Books.

Between these two publications Ovid had made his first appearance in England in Elizabeth's reign. In 1560 appeared *The fable of Ovid tretting of Narcissus, translated out of Latin into English metre, with a moral thereunto, very pleasaunte to rede*, by T. H. He was Thomas Howell, secretary successively to the Earl of Shrewsbury and the Countess of Pembroke, and a minor poet. His work was, in part, a rendering of ll. 342–510 of Book III of the *Metamorphoses*, telling the story of Narcissus, hopelessly beloved by the nymph Echo, and himself consumed by an equally hopeless passion for his own image reflected in a pool. Howell's version is in couplets of which the first line has six feet and the second has seven. Here is his translation of Narcissus's farewell words with Echo's repetition (' v ' replacing ' u ' and punctuation modified) :

Thus lokyng in the well, the last he spake was thys :
Alas ! thou ladde to much in vayne beloved of me a mys !
Whych selfe same wordes agayne this Ecco streight dyd yell,
And as Narcissus toke hys leve, she bad hym eke fayre well.

But the translation of about 170 Latin lines is made by Howell the occasion of, almost the excuse for, his own moralization of Ovid's fable of Narcissus in 127 rhyme-royal stanzas of seven lines each. After asking pardon for his youthful lack of skill Howell declares :

> I meane to shewe, according to my wytte,
> That Ovyd by this tale no follye mente.

and he adds this warning,

> Whiche Ovid now this Poete sure devine
> Doth collour in so wonderfull a sorte
> That such as twyse refuse to reade a lyne
> Wyth good advice, to make there wytte resorte
> To reasons schole, their Lessons to reporte,
> Shall never gather Ovids meanyng straunge
> That wysdome hydeth with some pleasaunt chaunge.

He then proceeds to expatiate on the fate of Narcissus as the result of overweening pride, and in characteristic Renaissance fashion cites other Biblical and Classical examples, beginning with Lucifer and ending with Cleopatra.

And he goes on improving the occasion till he finally asserts that by the metamorphosis of Narcissus into a flower Ovid intended to signify

> That youth and bewghte come and soone be paste
> Even as the flower that wetherithe full fast.

Two other versions of selected stories from the *Metamorphoses* followed in the same decade. In 1565 Thomas Peend of the Middle Temple produced *The pleasant fable of Hermaphroditus and Salmacis* (Book IV) of which the only copies are in the Bodleian and the Rylands library. In 1569 there came from the pen of William Hubbard, with a different appeal in the title, *The tragicall and lamentable historie of Ceyx, Kynge of Trachine and Alcione his wife* (Book XI). Of this the Bodleian has the only copy. In the same year Thomas Underdown published a translation of Ovid's *Invective against Ibis*.

The piecemeal excerpts from the *Metamorphoses* in the vernacular were eclipsed by the comprehensive undertaking of Arthur Golding, who in 1565 issued his translation of the first four Books of the poem, and in 1567 completed the version of all the fifteen Books. Like Howell he gave an enticing assurance that it was " a woorke very pleasant and delectable," accompanied by a warning :

> With skill, heede, and judgment thys woorke must be red,
> For els too the reader it stands in small stead.

Golding was born about 1536, and was connected by marriage with John de Vere, sixteenth Earl of Oxford. He wrote a " Discourse " upon the earthquake of April 6, 1580, but otherwise confined himself almost entirely to translations, in which he was prolific and versatile. They included, *inter alia*, various works of Calvin, Beza's tragedy,

Abraham's Sacrifice, Seneca's *Benefits*, Caesar's *Gallic War*, and the completion of Sir P. Sidney's version of de Mornay's *History of Christianity*. But it is on the *Metamorphoses* that his fame and influence chiefly rest. Its popularity is attested by the call for successive editions in 1575, 1587, 1603 and 1612. The modern reader who may find it difficult to cope with the closely printed black-letter text of the original publication has had his way smoothed by Dr W. H. D. Rouse in his handsome and scholarly edition issued by the De La More Press in 1904.

In the 1565 translation of the first four Books, Golding prefixed a prose dedication to the Earl of Leicester asking him to accept it as a New Year's gift. In the 1567 publication he substituted a long verse epistle to the Earl, declaring

> The woork is brought too end by which the author did account
> (And rightly) with eternal fame above the starres too mount,
> For whatsoever hath been writ of auncient tyme in greeke
> By sundry men dispersedly, and in the latin eke,
> Of this same dark Philosophie of turned shapes, the same
> Hath Ovid into one whole masse in this booke brought to fame.

Golding proceeds to summarize the stories in each of the Books, adding a moral interpretation of each, and then turns to forestall possible objectors.

> If any man will say theis things may better lerned bee
> Out of divine philosophie or scripture, I agree
> That nothing may in worthinesse with holy writ compare.
> Howbeit so farre foorth as things no whit impeachment are
> Too vertue and too godlynesse but furtherers of the same,
> I trust we may them saufly use without desert of blame.

So far, so good, but Golding's further appeal falls, at any rate to-day, on less responsive ears.

> What man is he but would suppose the author of this booke
> The first foundation of his woorke from Moyses wryghtings tooke ?
> Not only in effect he dooth with Genesis agree,
> But also in the order of creation, save that hee
> Makes no distinction of the dayes.

Golding then goes on to harmonize the Scriptural accounts of the Creation, Paradise and the Flood with what he takes to be their equivalents in the *Metamorphoses*. The Epistle to Leicester is followed by "the Preface to the Reader," in somewhat similar defensive and moralizing vein. And now that he has finished his labours, Golding claims that he has made of Ovid an English poet :

> And now I have him made so well acquainted with our toong,
> As that he may in English verse as in our own be soong,
> Wherein although for pleasant style I cannot make account
> Too match myne author, who in that all other dooth surmount,
> Yit (gentle Reader) I doo trust my travell in this cace
> May purchace favour in thy sight my dooings to embrace.

You will have noticed that my quotations from Golding's Epistle to Leicester and from the Preface to the Reader have been in the long fourteen-syllable line, and this is the metre that Golding uses to represent the Latin hexameter of the original from beginning to end. I think that something less than full justice is done in Charles Whibley's comment in Chapter I of Vol. IV of *The Cambridge History of English Literature.*

" The chief characteristic of the translation is its evenness. It never falls below or rises above a certain level. The craftsmanship is neither slovenly nor distinguished. The narrative flows through its easy channel without the smallest shock of interruption. In other words, the style is rapid, fluent and monotonous. The author is never a poet, and never a shirk."

I will quote in illustration of Golding's style two passages, both of which have an association interest. The first is part of Medea's appeal to the elemental powers to aid her when she is about to restore the youth of Jason's father. The lines are from Book VII, 197–206, beginning :

> Auraeque et venti, montesque, amnesque, lucusque,
> Dique omnes nemorum, dique omnes noctis adeste.

Golding's rendering is :

Ye Ayres and windes : ye Elves of Hilles, of Brookes, of Woods alone,
Of standing Lakes, and of the Night approche ye everychone.
Through helpe of whom (the crooked bankes much wondring at the thing)
I have compelled streames to run cleane backward to their spring.
By charmes I make the calme Seas rough, and make the rough Seas plaine,
And cover all the Skie with Cloudes and chase them thence againe.
By charmes I rayse and lay the windes and burst the Vipers jaw,
And from the bowels of the Earth both stones and trees doe drawe.
Whole woods and Forestes I remove ; I make the Mountaines shake,
And even the Earth it selfe to grone and fearfully to quake.
I call up dead men from their graves.

Compare with this the following :

Ye elves of hills, brookes, standing lakes, and groves . . .
               by whose aid—
Weak masters though ye be—I have bedimm'd
The noontide sun, call'd forth the mutinous winds,
And 'twixt the green sea and the azured vault
Set roaring war ; to the dread-rattling thunder
Have I given fire and rifted Jove's stout oak
With his own bolt ; the strong-based promontory
Have I made shake ; and by the spurs pluck'd up
The pine and cedar ; graves at my command
Have wak'd their sleepers, oped, and let men forth
By my so potent art.

Everyone will recognize that this is part of Prospero's speech before abjuring his " rough magic." That it was inspired by Golding's rendering of Medea's incantation is plain not only from the unmistakable verbal echoes but from the whole conception of magic being employed in both instances to reverse the natural order, even of life and death. Of course in the *Tempest* passage there are the added touches of Shakespearian imagination and melody.

My second excerpt is from the account in Book VIII of the visit of two of the gods to Philemon and Baucis in the Phrygian hill-country, beginning at l. 626,

> Juppiter huc specie mortali cumque parente
> Venit Atlantiades positis caducifer alis.

Here is Golding's version :

> The mightie *Jove* and *Mercurie* his sonne in shape of men
> Resorted thither on a tyme. A thousand houses when
> For roome too lodge in they had sought, a thousand houses bard
> Theyr doores against them. Neretheless one Cotage afterward
> Receyved them, and that was but a pelting one indeede.
> The roof thereof was thatched all with straw and fennish reede,
> Howbeet two honest auncient folke of whom she *Baucis* hight
> And he *Philemon*, in that Cote theyr fayth in youth had plight,
> And in that Cote had spent theyr age.

Now turn to *Much Ado about Nothing*, II, i, and the talk between Don Pedro and Hero at the masked ball :

D. Pedro. Lady, will you walk about with your friend ?
Hero. So you walk softly, and look sweetly, and say nothing, I am yours for the walk ; and especially when I walk away.
D. Pedro. With me in your company ?
Hero. I may say so, when I please.
D. Pedro. And when please you to say so ?
Hero. When I like your favour ; for God defend the lute should be like the case !
D. Pedro. My visor is Philemon's roof ; within the house is Jove.
Hero. Why, then, your visor should be thatch'd.
D. Pedro. Speak low, if you speak love.

Here, very unexpectedly, there is brought in a reference to Philemon's thatched roof, which the gallants and the groundlings in the Globe Theatre must have been remarkably " quick in the uptake " to appreciate. And Shakespeare's equally unlooked-for insertion into a long prose scene of a fourteener rhyming couplet is evidently in imitation of Golding.

There is another unexpected reference to the same episode at the beginning of Act III, ii, of *As You Like It*. When Touchstone condescendingly tells Audrey, " I am here with thee and thy goats, as the most capricious [fantastic] poet, honest Ovid, was among the Goths," Jacques exclaims, " O knowledge ill-inhabited, worse than Jove in a thatched house ! "

The mention of Ovid among the Goths shows that Shakespeare knew about the *Tristia* or at any rate about the conditions in which that poem was written. A couplet from the *Heroides* I, 35–6, beginning "Hac ibat Simois" is found in *The Taming of the Shrew*, III, i, 28 and another line II, 66 "Di faciant, laudis summa sit ista tuac" in *III Henry VI*, I, iii, 48. The second half of *Metamorphoses* I, 150, "Terras Astraea reliquit" comes in *Titus Andronicus*, IV, iii, 4. But even if one is not a 'disintegrator,' one may have doubts about the completely Shakespearian authorship of these plays. On the title page of *Venus and Adonis* there is a couplet from *Amores* I, xv, 35–6.

> Vilia miretur vulgus ; mihi flavus Apollo
> Pocula Castalia plena ministret aqua.

But this may have been affixed by the publisher, and the description of the boar in the poem, ll. 619 ff., as Dr Rouse has pointed out, recalls a passage in Golding's version, viii. 376. My own view, set forth in my 1943 Shakespeare Lecture to the British Academy, is that the dramatist's knowledge of the Classics in the original was very limited. However this may be, when Shakespeare puts into the mouth of Holofernes in *Love's Labour's Lost*, IV, ii, the punning eulogy, "Ovidius Naso was the man ; and why indeed, Naso, but for smelling out the odoriferous flowers of fancy, the jerks of invention ? " it was not the Ovid of the Classical Association, but the Ovid of Arthur Golding that was mainly in his mind.

In the same year, 1567, that Golding's complete *Metamorphoses* appeared there was issued a translation of the *Heroides* by George Turbervile with the title, *Heroycall Epistles*. Turbervile, born about 1540, was educated at Winchester and New College, Oxford. He was the author of a small book of poems, but like Golding he made his mark as a versatile translator. Among his English versions were the *Eclogues* of Mantuanus and *Tragical Tales* from Boccaccio and Bandello. But the *Heroycall Epistles* is his chief achievement. Though he speaks of it as a "trifling toye," it was a really formidable undertaking, for the twenty-one Epistles contain almost 4000 elegiac lines which are nearly doubled in Turbervile's English. This is not mainly due to freedom in translation but to Turbervile's use mainly of comparatively short lines. Unlike Golding he varies his metre. His favourite form is a four-line stanza, of which the first, second and fourth lines contain three feet and the third has four. He uses less frequently the more familiar four-line stanza with alternate four and three feet. And six of the Epistles are rendered, as Surrey had done with two Books of the *Aeneid*, into blank verse. Let me give an illustration of Turbervile's use of each of these three metres. In Epistle XIX, 9–16 beginning :

> Vos modo venando, modo rus geniale colendo,
> Ponitis in varia tempora longa mora,

Hero contrasts her lonely state with Leander's varied choice of occupations. Here is Turbervile's version :

> You men contrive the time
>   And loathsome tide away :
> Sometime in tillage of your soyles,
>   Sometime you hunt the day.
> Sometime at open barre
>   You pleade a clients case :
> To tennis now, and then with horse
>   You runne a lusty race.
> Sometime you pitch for foule,
>   For fish you lay your line ;
> And when the day is spent and gone,
>   You fall to quaffing wine.
> Now I can none of these,
>   Though lesser were my flame ;
> Thy Hero can do nothing els
>   But cleape her lovers name.

In Epistle V, ll. 13 ff., beginning :

> Saepe greges inter requievimus arbore tecti,
>   Mixtaque cum foliis praebuit herba forum,

Oenone reminds Paris of their former rural joys. Turbervile thus translates :

> How oft have we in shaddow layne
>   Whilst hungry flocks have fed ?
> How oft have we of grasse and groaves
>   Prepard a homely bed ?
> How oft on simple stacks of straw
>   And bennet did we rest ?
> I sundry times have helpe to pitch
>   Thy wyles for want of ayde,
> And prest thy houndes to climbe the hills
>   That gladly would have stay'd.
> The boysteous Beech Oenons name
>   In outward barke doth beare ;
> And with thy carving knife is cut
>   Oenon every where.

In Epistle XII, ll. 31–36, beginning :

> Tunc ego te vidi, tunc coepi scire quis esses,
>   Illa fuit mentis prima ruina meae,

Medea reminds Jason of how she first became enamoured of him. This is Turbervile's blank-verse reading :

> Then saw I thee and perisht eke inflamed
> With fire unknowne, and fried with straungie gleade,
> As fore the Aultars burnes the torch of Pyne.
> Both featurde well thou were and fates me drew ;

> Thine eyes my dazeled lights did ravish quite
> Which quickly thou discridste. For who may well
> Keep love in mewe, that no man it discerne ?
> Ay flame it selfe by casting light, bewrayes.

These are, I think, favourable examples of Turbervile's style in his different metres. He is at his best when, as in my two first quotations, he is turning Ovid's concrete details, with some elaboration, into racy, picturesque English. In quest of this Turbervile employs a diversified and sometimes outlandish vocabulary, e.g., in the above extracts, ' cleape ' =call, ' bennet '=grass-stalk, ' boysteous '=rough, ' gleade '=flame. He is less happy when, as often, he uses words that are colloquial or have undignified association, e.g. ' fist ' for hand, ' brat ' for child, ' smack ' for kiss. And partly owing to the discrepancies between synthetic Latin and analytical English he often fails to reproduce Ovid's deliberate and pointed balance. That he himself realized the difficulties of his task is plain from the confession in his Epilogue.

> He shall find he hath a Crow to pull
> That undertakes with well agreeing File
> Of English verse to rub the Romans stile.

All the more therefore

> it is a worke of prayse to cause
> A Romane borne to speake with English jawes.

That Turbervile's contemporaries found it a " worke of prayse " is evident from the fact that after 1567 four later editions were called for of which the last was in 1600. If one cannot point to any link between the *Heroycall Epistles* and an Elizabethan literary figure as definite as that between Golding's *Metamorphoses* and Shakespeare, yet its influence in making the heroines of Greek legend and their lovers generally familiar must have been far-reaching. But after 1600 it was not reprinted till 1928 when the Cresset Press published a finely illustrated *édition de luxe* of which it was my privilege to be the editor.

A writer with more original work to his credit than any hitherto mentioned entered the field of Ovid translation when Thomas Churchyard in 1572 published his version of the first three Books of the *Tristia*. He had made something of a mark with his contribution to *A Mirror for Magistrates* in 1563 of the ' tragedy ' of *Shore's Wife*. He had served as a soldier in Scotland, Ireland and on the Continent, and had afterwards with little success sought to advance his fortunes as a hanger-on to the Court and the nobility. It may well have been the sense of frustration in his own career that prompted him to translate the most mournful of Ovid's works. But there is nothing to this effect in his curious dedication of his version to Sir Christopher Hatton. In it he makes no direct mention of Ovid but apologizes to Hatton for presenting him with

" another man's worke . . . sufficient to purchase good report," instead of his intended collection of *Churchyard's Chips*, a miscellaneous volume which saw the light in 1575. Like Golding, Churchyard used throughout the rhymed 'fourteener,' though this is less suited to the elegiac metre of the *Tristia* than the hexameters of the *Metamorphoses*. As a specimen I quote his translation of the lines (II, 327 ff.) beginning :

> Arguor immerito : tenuis mihi campus aratur ;
> Illud erat magnae fertilitatis opus.

in which Ovid replies to the charge that he ought to have dealt in his verse with the war against Troy, or the victories of Rome or the exploits of Augustus himself :

> As rightfully I am reprovde, in barren fielde I tilde,
> That noble worke is far more large, with greater plenty fielde.
> For though the slender boate is bould in smaller streame to play,
> Yet like disport it dareth not in surging seas assay.
> And doubtinge that for greater things my minde is farre unfit,
> In dittyes small it may suffice that I do shew my wit.
> But if thou should commaund to tell of Giantes grevous wounds,
> Which they thrugh fyre of Jove did feele, the worke my wit confounds.
> A fruitfull minde it doth requyre of Caesars actes to wright,
> Least els perhappes with matter much the worke may want his right,
> Which though I durst have take in hand, yet dreading much amonge,
> Thy noble power I might abate, which were too great a wronge,
> To lighter worke I therefore went, and youthfull verse addrest
> With fayned love a care I had to feede my ficcle brest.

This is jog-trot verse, with a superfluity of monosyllables and in parts not lucid. Of the 1572 edition there is only one surviving copy in the British Museum, and this is imperfect, lacking the last pages, signature ' D.' But the translation found a public, for two more editions were issued in 1578 and 1580. The 1578 quarto is also extant in a single copy, formerly in Lord Spencer's Althorp library, from which it was reprinted in 1816 for the Roxburghe Club. It is now in the Manchester Rylands library, while the two surviving 1580 copies are in the Bodleian and the Huntington libraries.

To the translators already mentioned has now to be added an Elizabethan of the first rank, Christopher Marlowe. Four editions of his version of *Ovid's Elegies, three Books* and two of *Certain of Ovid's Elegies* were issued together, in every case, with *Epigrams* by Sir John Davies. All the editions were undated and the imprint on the title page of Middleburgh (in Holland) as the place of publication was almost certainly spurious. The so-called *Elegies* are the three Books of the *Amores*, and the presumption is that the translation dates from some time during Marlowe's Cambridge career, between 1581–87. A young scholar of his glowing temper would be attracted not only by the erotic elements in Ovid's poem but by its rich mythological lore. It is true, as I have

said elsewhere, that Marlowe would not have got full marks in a scholar-
ship examination.   He made a number of 'howlers.'   Thus the line
" Ipse locus nemorum canebat frugibus Ide,' i.e. " Ida the seat of groves
was white with harvest " is rendered " Ida the seat of groves did sing
with corn," where Marlowe mistook ' cānebat ' for ' cănebat.'   Again
the invocation " linguis animisque favete," i.e. " keep silence and
attend " is turned into " themselves let all men cheer."   On the other
hand a number of apparent inaccuracies or obscurities are due either
to changes in the meaning of words or to differences between the
Elizabethan Latin texts of Ovid and those now in use.   And it is to
Marlowe's credit that he tried faithfully to render every Latin line into
its English equivalent.   This was all the more difficult because unlike
the previous translators of Ovid he had not given himself additional
elbow-room.   His metre was the rhyming couplet of five-foot lines,
where ten feet replaced the eleven feet of the Latin elegiac couplet.   The
compression sometimes led to awkwardness, but on the other hand it
emabled Marlowe at times to reproduce the balance and terseness of the
original as none of the previous translators had done, e.g.

> Et celer admissus labitur annus equis.
> And with swift horses the swift year soon leaves us.

and

> Quo lapis exiguus par sibi carmen habet.
> The little stones these little verses have.

Except for occasional colloquialisms which remind us of Turbervile,
Marlowe's vocabulary is well-chosen and varied, and he avoids the
excessive alliteration favoured by most Elizabethan translators.   His
versification is uneven and betrays something of the prentice hand, but
at its best it foreshadows his later mastery of metre.   Thus he translates
in Book I, Elegy 13, Ovid's appeal to Aurora to delay her coming :

> Whither runn'st thou that men and women love not ?
> Hold in thy rosy horses that they move not.
> Ere thou rise, stars teach seamen where to sail,
> But when thou comest, they of their courses fail.
> Poor travellers, though tir'd, rise at thy sight,
> And soldiers make them ready to the fight.
> The painful hind by thee to field is sent ;
> Slow oxen early in the yoke are pent.
> Thou cozen'st boys of sleep, and dost betray them
> To pedants that with cruel lashes pay them.

It is, as will be remembered, a later line from the same elegy, slightly
varied from its original form, " O lente, lente currite noctis equi," that
bursts so movingly from Faustus's lips as his dread doom draws nigh.
   And here is the version of some of the lines in Book I, Elegy 15, in
which the poet prophesies his eternal fame :

Therefore when flint and iron wear away,
Verse is immortal and shall ne'er decay.
To verse let kings give place and kingly shows,
And banks o'er which gold-bearing Tagus flows.

.   .   .   .

The living, not the dead can envy bite,
For after death all men receive their right.
Then though death rakes my bones in funeral fire
I'll live, and as he pulls me down, mount higher.

If two highly placed prelates had fully had their way, Marlowe's translation of the *Amores* would not have contributed either to Ovid's immortality or his own. For by an order of the Archbishop of Canterbury and the Bishop of London the volumes containing the *Elegies* and Davies's *Epigrams* were publicly burnt with other books on June 4, 1599. But fortunately one or two copies of what appear to be the earliest editions escaped the flames, and their text is available to-day in the original spelling in Tucker Brooke's *Marlowe* and in modernized spelling in Bullen's *Marlowe* and L. C. Martin's edition of Marlowe's *Poems*.

It was not, however, through translations only that Ovid's influence was felt. His mastery of poetic narrative inspired a number of Elizabethan achievements in the same field. Thus Francis Meres testifies in 1598 " the sweet, witty soul of Ovid lives in mellifluous and honey-tongued Shakespeare, witness his *Venus and Adonis*, his *Lucrece*, his sugared sonnets." Though Musaeus was the main source of Marlowe's *Hero and Leander* it is full of Ovidian echoes. And we have other echoes in such titles as Lodge's *Scilla's Metamorphosis* (1589), Marston's *The Metamorphosis of Pygmalion's Image* (1598), Harrington's unseemly *Metamorphosis of Ajax* (1599) and Tourneur's *The Transformed Metamorphosis* (1600).

But by far the most elaborate work with a *Metamorphosis* title still remains unpublished. It is *The Newe Metamorphosis* written by J. M., gent., and dated 1600. It is contained in three quarto volumes (B.M. Addit. MSS., 14,824–14,826) and includes twenty-four Books. A study of it by Dr J. H. H. Lyon, with selections from the MS., was issued from the Columbia University Press in 1919. Lyon has shown, if internal evidence can be trusted, that J. M. was Jervis Markham, who thus in his Prologue describes his poetic miscellany and his Classical model :

Even as a Flemish Galleymaufrey made
Of flesh, herbes, onyons, both of roote and blade,
So shall you fynde them in this booke conteinde
For some strange things to write I onely ay'mde.
I ne're sawe any of our Nation yet
That me a patterne in this subiecte set,
Nor but one stranger, Ovid alone was he
That in this labour did incourage me.

There could be no more explicit acknowledgment of a debt, and in a number of his tales, especially those relating the amours of various classical gods and in the transformations with which many of the stories close, the direct influence of Ovid is manifest. But though the MS. is dated 1600 the allusions in it to Prince Henry's death in 1612 and to Ralegh's *History of the World* published in 1614 prove that Markham must have been adding to it for many years. Thus, though originally planned according to its first sub-title as "A Feaste of Fancie of Poeticall Legendes," it was extended to include satirical, topical, and autobiographical features which carry us very far from Augustan Rome.

But now let us return there under the guidance of two major Elizabethans, George Chapman and Ben Jonson. To both of them the tradition of Ovid's relations with an imperial Julia, in their eyes the daughter, not the granddaughter, of Augustus, furnished material upon which they worked in very different fashion. Among Chapman's earlier writings is the curious poem *Ovid's Banquet of Sence*, published in 1595. According to the 'argument' which prefaces the poem, Ovid conceals himself in a garden of the emperor's court where Julia, whom he calls Corinna, was bathing. This gives him the opportunity of gratifying each of his senses in turn. While bathing, Corinna plays upon her lute and sings and thus enchants her lover's sense of hearing. Then the odours or perfumes which she used in her bath satisfied his sense of smell. Thereafter he ventured " to see her in the pride of her nakednesse " and " discovered the comfort hee conceived in seeing, and the glorie of her beautie." He is then emboldened to ask for a kiss to gratify his sense of taste, and after some demur she consents.

> Ovid (sayd shee) I am well pleased to yield ;
> Beautie by vertue cannot be abusde ;
>   Nor will I coylie lyft Minervas shielde
> Against Minerva, honor is not brusde
>   With such a tender pressure as a kisse,
> Nor yielding soone to words, though seldome vsde ;
>   Nicenesse in civill favours folly is :
> Long sutes make never good a bad detection,
> Nor yielding soone makes bad a good affection.

Finally to crown the banquet Ovid begs that he may gratify the " sences Emperor, Sweet Feeling." But before this can be consummated they are interrupted and the poem comes to an abrupt conclusion. As Miss Bartlett has suggested, Chapman probably found it difficult to round off this paradoxical effort of " an erotic poem founded in the Neoplatonic doctrine of love. . . . The doctrine is that man must partake to the full of sensual contentment in order that his mind may be excited to a higher love."

Chapman had thus brought Ovid and Julia to life again in amorous dialogue. There was only one further step to be taken, to exhibit them in speech and motion on the Elizabethan stage. This was the achievement of Ben Jonson in *The Poetaster* (1601). In the opening scene Ovid is seen perusing the 15th Elegy of Book I of the *Amores*, in which he predicts immortality for his poetry, and of which Jonson gives an English version slightly different from Marlowe's, part of which I have quoted. His father who has destined him for the law bursts in furiously :

" Is this the scope and aim of thy studies ? Are these the hopeful courses wherewith I have so long flattered my expectations from thee ? Verses ! poetry ! "

Ovid in vain seeks to calm him, and his farewell injunction is, " If thou wilt hold my favour abandon these idle studies that so bewitch thee . . . and look only forward to the law." As he goes out fuming, a fellow poet of Ovid, Tibullus, enters with an invitation to him from Princess Julia to meet her at the house of Albius, a jeweller. Here there is a gay party in which only Propertius still mourning the loss of his Cynthia is a discordant sombre figure. This is a prelude to later more daring revels in which the company headed by Ovid as Jupiter and Julia as Juno impersonate the Roman deities. News of this is brought to Augustus, who enters to stop the masquerade and to send Julia to prison and Ovid to perpetual banishment. Before they serve their sentences, in a scene that irresistibly recalls the parting of Romeo and Juliet, Julia appears at her chamber window to take a lingering farewell of her lover below :

> *Julia.* Ovid, my love, alas may we not stay
>   A little longer (think'st thou) undiscerned ?
> *Ovid.* For thine own good, fair Goddess, do not stay.
>
> .   .   .   .
>
> *Julia.* I will be gone then and not heaven itself
>   Shall draw me back.
> *Ovid.*   Yet, Julia, if thou wilt,
>   A little longer stay.
> *Julia.*   I am content.

But he remembers that " if both stay, both die," and he flings away with Julia's image in his heart.

And I would ask you to note that this is not only the exit of Ovid from the Rome of Augustus but virtually from the London of Elizabeth. Except for a version of the episode of Salmacis and Hermaphroditus, assigned to Francis Beaumont in 1602, neither in translation nor otherwise did Ovid figure again before the Queen's death on March 24, 1603. For details of the further flow of translations before the Civil War, in which W. Saltonstall and George Sandys have conspicuous parts, I would refer you to the *Short-Title Catalogue*. The Elizabethan period, in its strict limits, has yielded material enough for this afternoon's survey. We have found fruitful contacts between Publius Ovidius Naso and Elizabethans of the front rank, Marlowe, Shakespeare, Chapman, Ben

Jonson ; also with reputable figures of lesser degree, Golding, Turbervile and Churchyard, as well as such minor personages as Howell, Hubbard and Peend. And behind these stand the great nameless company of readers who bought up so eagerly the editions that followed one another from the press.

Thus Ovid's influence was widespread and, I would claim, beneficial. Of course Howell was on the wrong tack when he exalted him as a moralist and still more Golding when he drew a parallel between him and the author of *Genesis*. At the opposite extreme were the prelates who consigned Marlowe's translation of the *Amores* to the flames. They on their part overestimated the demoralizing effect of a work of which so much was outside the ken of Elizabethan Londoners. And it is to be noted that while the *Metamorphoses*, the *Heroides* and the *Tristia* were turned into English there was no Elizabethan vernacular version of the *Ars Amatoria*.

But it is outside the sphere of morals that Ovid's really pervasive influence is to be traced. He spread before the eyes of the Elizabethans an enthralling wealth of mythological and legendary lore. It is true, as some American scholars have recently emphasized, that much of this is to be found in contemporary encyclopaedic dictionaries. But what they contained in dry outline was presented in glowing imaginative life in Ovid's pages. This made a direct appeal to the exuberant Elizabethan temper. At the same time Ovid's artistic, at times over-artificial, verse-technique had a valuable controlling and chastening influence. Redundancy and excess were constant temptations of the Elizabethans. We have seen how they affected Golding's and Turbervile's translations. Nevertheless they made conscious efforts to fall as little as might be below the linguistic and rhythmical standard set by their Latin model.

Marlowe by his natural instinct succeeded better, but even he profited by the discipline thereby involved. And Shakespeare himself echoed in one of his loftiest and latest utterances lines from the *Metamorphoses*. Does not our survey of Ovid and the Elizabethans go far to confirm Dr Mackail's dictum. " He was not a poet of the first order ; yet few poets of the first order have done a work of such wide importance " ?